MARTIN BAXENDALE'S

BETTER SEX GUIDE

INTRODUCTION

I've personally tried every idea in this book, and it's certainly spiced up <u>my</u> sex life! I hope it does the same for you.

MARTIN BAXENDALE

(Note: Please send all fan-mail and/or love letters to: Martin Baxendale, The High-Security Ward, National Hospital For The Treatment of Bizarre Sexual Behaviour, Wobbling-by-the-Sea, Sussex, England)

P.S. <u>Mrs</u> Baxendale here: I don't know <u>who</u> Martin has tried all these ideas with, but it certainly wasn't <u>me</u> (well, apart from the bit about having sex in the giant squirrel costumes in the park) and I'll be starting divorce proceedings immediately.

FOREPLAY AND G-SPOTS

FOREPLAY: Most men are now fully aware of women's needs for prolonged and varied foreplay prior to sex. Unfortunately, many of us are still pretty crap at it and find it awfully tiring and time-consuming.

Personally, I favour <u>mechanising</u> and <u>automating</u> the whole business as much as possible (see illustration).

Rubber foreplay glove with battery-operated vibrating fiddling finger.

Battery-operated vibrating toe extension.

Foreplay tool-kit, containing assorted vibrators and other tickling, tweaking, twiddling and vacuum-sucking sex aids (plus lots of spare long-life batteries).

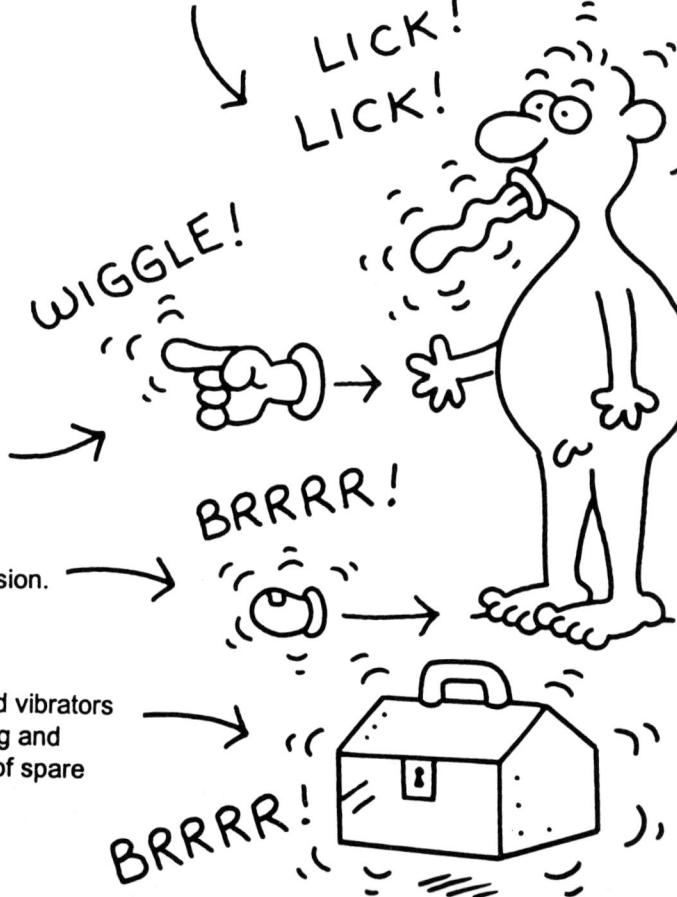

Battery-operated tongue extension.

LICK! LICK!

WIGGLE!

BRRRR!

BRRRR!

THE FEMALE G-SPOT: If the man gets <u>very</u> bored during prolonged foreplay, he can always while away the time searching for his partner's G-spot, the source of previously undiscovered heights of pleasure for the woman (although some say the G-spot is a myth perpetuated by the publishers of illustrated gynaecology books and the manufacturers of rubber pencil torches).

Personally, I found Mrs Baxendale's G-spot down the back of our settee cushions.

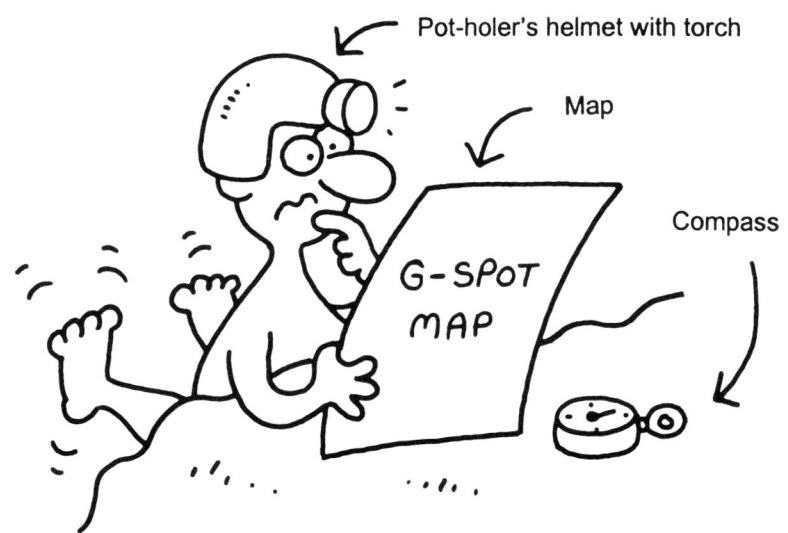

Pot-holer's helmet with torch

Map

Compass

G-SPOT MAP

THE MALE G-SPOT: An exciting competition from the publishers of this guide book:

We are offering a generous prize of 50p worth of sex-shop gift vouchers for the first reader to locate the (as yet undiscovered) <u>male</u> G-spot. Here are some hints:

Is it most likely to be:
A) Up his bottom?
B) Up his nose?
C) Just behind his left testicle?

Good hunting girls, and you can buy your surgical gloves, tweezers and rubber pencil torches from our website, www.male-G-spot-search.com.

BE ADVENTUROUS IN THE BEDROOM

Instead of the same boring old stuff, why not try something new in the bedroom? Start by trying new positions, approaches and techniques, such as the following:

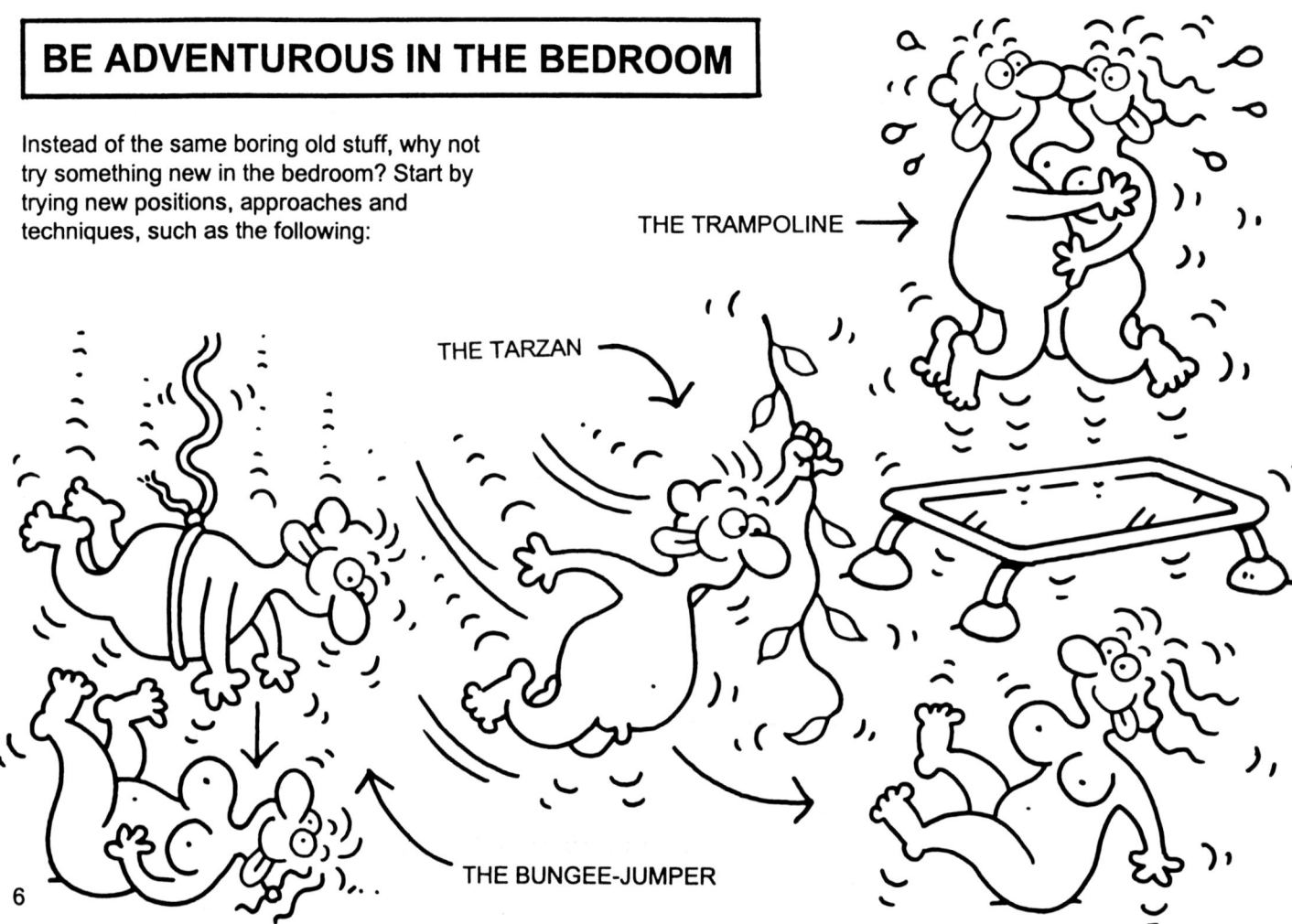

THE TRAMPOLINE →

THE TARZAN

THE BUNGEE-JUMPER

6

THE TRAPEZE

THE HUMAN CANNON-BALL

7

SPREAD IT ON AND LICK IT OFF:

Everyone's heard of the erotic appeal of licking cream, chocolate sauce, etc. off your loved one, but have you actually tried it?

Between you and me, it's not just sexy, it's also brilliant if you're feeling both randy and a bit peckish. And if you're supposed to be on a diet, it's a great excuse to binge on cream and choccy sauce in a good cause!

My personal favourites include (in addition to the essential whipped cream and choc sauce) peanut butter, marmalade, HP brown sauce, marmite, and cold baked beans.

Skimpy silk thong.

Smelly socks.

Baggy Y-fronts.

CROSS-DRESSING:
This can be a bit of a turn-on for some people, occasionally slipping into your partner's undies for a change.

Personally, I've grown very fond of Mrs Baxendale's thongs. But for some reason she's never been so keen on wearing my underwear. Strange!

BONDAGE FOR WIMPS:
If, like me, you're a bit of a scaredy-cat who's not too keen on being tied up for real, try this easy-escape approach to sexy bondage in the bedroom:

Tie hands and feet to bed-ends with soggy cooked spaghetti.

Edible liquorice handcuffs.

Whip made with soggy spaghetti.

Bolognese sauce and parmesan cheese for mixing with left-over spaghetti for a tasty post-sex snack.

9

SEXY UNIFORMS: Dressing up in a sexy uniform is often a good way to turn your partner on, but only if you choose the right kind of uniform:

√ **RIGHT!**
NURSE.

√ **RIGHT!**
NAVAL OFFICER.

√ **RIGHT!**
FRENCH MAID.

X **WRONG!**
ZOO-KEEPER.

X **WRONG!**
BURGER-FRIER.

Smelling of elephant-pooh.

Smelling of burgers.

EROTIC DANCES: A slow teasing strip or other erotic dance routine in the privacy of your bedroom before sex can be very arousing. Why not try it?

TANTRIC SEX: A mystical New-Age type sexual technique based on yoga-like concentration and control to prolong sex for hours and hours on end.

Only trouble is, last week I missed all my favourite programmes on TV. And Mrs Baxendale says all she wants is for it to last a bit longer than three minutes, and if she has to have sex with me for <u>that</u> long again, she's leaving me.

NOTE: Men, do try not to <u>fart</u> during the essential lap-dancing finale or you'll completely ruin the effect (Mrs Baxendale wouldn't speak to me for days after my unfortunate wind-breaking episode. Damned baked beans!)

11

THREESOMES: This can seem like an appealing idea to some people, but bear in mind that you and your partner might not have quite the same thing in mind:

↓

I FANCY A THREESOME!

① ME TOO!

② THAT NIGHT...

③

SAFER THREESOMES:
Having a threesome can also be difficult emotionally for one or both partners, even if they fancy it sexually; and group sex obviously carries the possibility of serious health risks these days. So here is my suggestion for a safer option:

Inflatable female sex doll.

Inflatable male sex doll.

HUH! JUST LIKE YOU!

Springing a leak.

WILT!

FARP!

13

BUT NOT JUST IN THE BEDROOM

SEX IN THE BATH: This is often suggested as both relaxing and sexy, with lots of sex-drive boosting aromatherapy candles and bath oils.

Watch you don't inadvertently get your willy stuck up the tap in all the confusion of the bubbles and the slippery splashing around (you should have seen the look the plumber gave <u>me</u> when we had to call him out).

Sensuous aromatherapy bath bubbles.

Snorkel.

Sensuous aromatherapy candle.

SEX IN THE GARDEN:

Having sex outdoors always feels a bit "naughty", so of course is a real turn-on. In the countryside you're usually okay - just find a quiet field or patch of woodland and you're away. But what if you fancy a quicky out in the garden on a warm summer's evening?

The last thing you want is to be spotted by nosey neighbours. So I've found the following disguise very useful (just freeze if your neighbours see you, and wait 'till they've gone before you carry on):

Disguise yourselves as "rude" garden gnomes.

SEX IN THE PARK: Sex outdoors in <u>public</u> <u>places</u> like the park, where you just might get caught is even "naughtier" and still more of a turn-on. But you don't actually <u>want</u> to get caught of course, so here's another handy disguise idea that I've used very successfully many times.

Dressed-up in squirrel costumes.

Short-sighted old dear.

COME AND GET YOUR PEANUTS!

16

Alternatively, you can paint yourselves all over with grey body-paint and pretend to be statues (don't forget to stay absolutely still whenever someone walks past).

Portable wooden statue plinth painted stone-gray.

Plaque that reads: Rodin's "The Shaggers".

TWEET TWEET!

TWEET!

Up against a tree is a favourite spot for an outdoor quickie, and that's okay out in the countryside; but in a busy park you're better nipping up the tree, where you're less likely to be seen.

Best to practise your bird-calls in case anyone spots the shaking branches and falling leaves. But beware - this may attract bird-watchers!

SEX AT THE BEACH:

Here again the problem (apart from sandy genitals) is how to have sex without being seen by the hundreds of other holidaymakers on the beach.

The answer is to get in the water, and to ensure that everyone else gets <u>out</u> of the water by wearing the appropriate costumes as you make love in the waves.

Shark costumes will ensure no-one comes near you in the sea, so the two of you can bob up and down together as rampantly and obscenely as you like.

SEX IN PHOTO-BOOTHS:

The bonus here is that you also get <u>photos</u> of yourselves having sex in a public place, as a memento of your naughty antics.

But do remember to take the pics from the slot when you leave. You don't want some little old lady having a heart-attack when she goes to get her photos.

Note: These photographs are <u>not</u> suitable for passport applications.

SEX IN A LIFT: This is a common fantasy, but few people actually do it because of the high risk of getting caught.

No problem! Just blow up this inflatable dummy "fat bloke" to block the lift entrance and make it look crowded, so no-one will get in, and you can shag happily away at the back of the lift totally undisturbed.

OH, YES! YES! YES! OH YES !!!

THRRRP!

Leaky air valve with built-in "fart" noise will further discourage people from getting in.

19

COMFY SEX IN A PUBLIC PLACE:

If you fancy naughty sex in a public place but with all the comfort of sex in a nice warm bed, then head for the beds department of your nearest furniture mega-store.

If a shopper walks past, remember to freeze and pretend to be shop-window dummies demonstrating the comfort of the beds for sale.

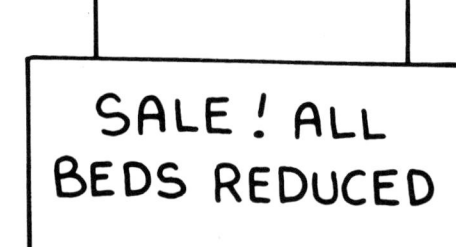

SALE ! ALL BEDS REDUCED

Pretending to be a display dummy.

SNORE!

SALE PRICE £300

SEX IN A RESTAURANT:

The problem here is <u>reaching</u> your partner under the table. Here are a couple of ideas.

Shoe with battery-operated extending vibrating toe.

BRRRR!

Inflatable dummy of yourself. Blow it up when no-one is looking, place it in your seat, and dive under the table to pleasure your partner.

SEX IN RESTAURANT TOILET:

Choose a posh restaurant with nice toilets (the Ladies is usually cleanest) and make sure you have the following with you:

Sign for toilet door, to discourage people from disturbing you.

OUT OF ORDER

SPLLRRP! SPLLRRP! SPLLRRP!

Just in case someone still comes into the loos, tape recorder with extra-loud and revolting diarrhoea poohing noises, to cover up the sounds of your love-making in the cubicle.

SEX ON THE MOVE: Sex and speed are an exciting mix, but trying to have sex in a fast-moving car can be very dangerous indeed.

Here are some safer alternatives, guaranteed to give you a combined sex/adrenalin high without waking up in the morgue with a tag on your toe and your willy in a separate bag.

Sex on roller-blades.

Sex on a skateboard.

CRASH!

And of course, if you get caught having sex in a public place, then you can always have a quicky in the back of the speeding <u>police</u> <u>van</u> as they take you away to the cells.

Sex on a bicycle.

SEX IN THE SKY:

Joining the "mile-high club" (having sex in the toilet on an airliner) is increasingly popular. But it's expensive and you're only likely to indulge when you go on holiday.

A cheaper everyday alternative is to nip down to the nearest funfair and hop on the flying aeroplanes roundabout ride for 50p.

SEX AND DANGEROUS SPORTS:

Having sex while taking part in dangerous sports (e.g. sky-diving, bob-sleigh racing, snowboarding, etc) can be very exciting.

But if attempting sex while sky-diving, do take care when frantically tearing your clothes off, not to inadvertently rip off your <u>parachutes</u> as well.

23

PLAYING SEXY GAMES

Even an old favourite like strip poker can add a bit of fun to your sex life. But whatever you do, don't try strip chess.

I did once, trying to be a bit posh and intellectual, and it took us over four hours just to get down to our undies.

ACTING OUT FANTASIES: This is an excellent way to add spice to your sex life. Here is just a small selection of some of my favourites:

FIREMAN RESCUES WOMAN FROM BLAZING BUILDING.

FISHERMAN RESCUES MERMAID FROM STORMY WATERS.

NAUGHTY PHONE-CALLS:

It can be fun to make sexy phone-calls to your loved one during the day, indulging in rude sex-talk with them while they're at work etc, to get them in the mood for when you both get home.

BEING SEXY STRANGERS:

The idea here is that you arrange to meet your partner somewhere (bar, nightclub, etc) and pretend to be strangers, who end up having a very sexy brief encounter.

"Disguise" yourselves in new sexy clothes, new perfume/aftershave, even a wig.

But watch you don't make your disguises <u>too</u> good, otherwise you could both end up making embarrassing mistakes.

A variation on the "sexy strangers" game is for the woman to dress in her sexiest, tartiest clothes and hang around in the street waiting to be picked up by her bloke.

WARNING: Best to avoid places where <u>real</u> tarts tend to hang out - men are easily confused.

MAKE YOUR OWN PORNO
FILM: This can be good sexy fun, and with the advent of cheap video cameras many couples have given it a go.

Remember, to give that authentic porno-film feel, you must come up with a totally crap storyline, full of unbelievable dialogue, just like the real thing.

31